Cruise Journal

NAME

ADDRESS

E-MAIL ADDRESS

WEBSITE

PHONE   FAX

EMERGENCY CONTACT PERSON

PHONE   FAX

AF358629

Day # .... Place ....

DATE

TEMPERATURE

☐ PORT ☐ AT SEA

SHIPBOARD ACTIVITIES LIST

FOOD AND DRINKS

PLANS FOR TODAY

1. ....
2. ....
3. ....

MY BEST EXPERIENCE TODAY

EVENING EVENTS

NEW FRIENDS

NOTES

Day # .... Place ....

DATE

TEMPERATURE

☐ PORT   ☐ AT SEA

SHIPBOARD ACTIVITIES LIST

FOOD AND DRINKS

PLANS FOR TODAY

1. ....
2. ....
3. ....

MY BEST EXPERIENCE TODAY

EVENING EVENTS

NEW FRIENDS

NOTES

Day # .... Place ....

DATE

TEMPERATURE

☐ PORT ☐ AT SEA

SHIPBOARD ACTIVITIES LIST

FOOD AND DRINKS

PLANS FOR TODAY

1. ....
2. ....
3. ....

MY BEST EXPERIENCE TODAY

EVENING EVENTS

NEW FRIENDS

NOTES

Day # .... Place ....

DATE

TEMPERATURE

☐ PORT ☐ AT SEA

SHIPBOARD ACTIVITIES LIST

FOOD AND DRINKS

PLANS FOR TODAY

1. ....
2. ....
3. ....

MY BEST EXPERIENCE TODAY

EVENING EVENTS

NEW FRIENDS

NOTES

Day #   Place

DATE

TEMPERATURE

☐ PORT   ☐ AT SEA

SHIPBOARD ACTIVITIES LIST

FOOD AND DRINKS

PLANS FOR TODAY

1.
2.
3.

MY BEST EXPERIENCE TODAY

EVENING EVENTS

NEW FRIENDS

NOTES

Day # .... Place ....

DATE

TEMPERATURE

☐ PORT   ☐ AT SEA

SHIPBOARD ACTIVITIES LIST

FOOD AND DRINKS

PLANS FOR TODAY

1. ....
2. ....
3. ....

MY BEST EXPERIENCE TODAY

EVENING EVENTS

NEW FRIENDS

NOTES

Day # .... Place ....

DATE

TEMPERATURE

☐ PORT   ☐ AT SEA

SHIPBOARD ACTIVITIES LIST

FOOD AND DRINKS

PLANS FOR TODAY

1. ....
2. ....
3. ....

MY BEST EXPERIENCE TODAY

EVENING EVENTS

NEW FRIENDS

NOTES

Day # .... Place ....

DATE

TEMPERATURE

☐ **PORT**   ☐ **AT SEA**

SHIPBOARD ACTIVITIES LIST

FOOD AND DRINKS

PLANS FOR TODAY

1. ....
2. ....
3. ....

MY BEST EXPERIENCE TODAY

EVENING EVENTS

NEW FRIENDS

NOTES

Day # .... Place ....

DATE

TEMPERATURE

☐ PORT ☐ AT SEA

SHIPBOARD ACTIVITIES LIST

FOOD AND DRINKS

PLANS FOR TODAY

1. ....
2. ....
3. ....

MY BEST EXPERIENCE TODAY

EVENING EVENTS

NEW FRIENDS

NOTES

Day # .... Place ....

DATE

TEMPERATURE

☐ PORT ☐ AT SEA

SHIPBOARD ACTIVITIES LIST

FOOD AND DRINKS

PLANS FOR TODAY

1. ....
2. ....
3. ....

MY BEST EXPERIENCE TODAY

EVENING EVENTS

NEW FRIENDS

NOTES

Day # .... Place ....

DATE

TEMPERATURE

☐ PORT   ☐ AT SEA

SHIPBOARD ACTIVITIES LIST

FOOD AND DRINKS

PLANS FOR TODAY

1. ....
2. ....
3. ....

MY BEST EXPERIENCE TODAY

EVENING EVENTS

NEW FRIENDS

NOTES

Day # .... Place ....

DATE

TEMPERATURE

☐ **PORT**   ☐ **AT SEA**

SHIPBOARD ACTIVITIES LIST

FOOD AND DRINKS

PLANS FOR TODAY

1. ....
2. ....
3. ....

MY BEST EXPERIENCE TODAY

EVENING EVENTS

NEW FRIENDS

NOTES

Day # .... Place ....

DATE

TEMPERATURE

☐ **PORT**   ☐ **AT SEA**

SHIPBOARD ACTIVITIES LIST

FOOD AND DRINKS

PLANS FOR TODAY

1. ....
2. ....
3. ....

MY BEST EXPERIENCE TODAY

EVENING EVENTS

NEW FRIENDS

NOTES

Day # .... Place ....

DATE

TEMPERATURE

☐ **PORT**   ☐ **AT SEA**

SHIPBOARD ACTIVITIES LIST

FOOD AND DRINKS

PLANS FOR TODAY

1. ....
2. ....
3. ....

MY BEST EXPERIENCE TODAY

EVENING EVENTS

NEW FRIENDS

NOTES

Day # .... Place ....

DATE

TEMPERATURE

☐ PORT ☐ AT SEA

SHIPBOARD ACTIVITIES LIST

FOOD AND DRINKS

PLANS FOR TODAY

1. ....
2. ....
3. ....

MY BEST EXPERIENCE TODAY

EVENING EVENTS

NEW FRIENDS

NOTES

Day # .... Place ....

DATE

TEMPERATURE

☐ PORT   ☐ AT SEA

SHIPBOARD ACTIVITIES LIST

FOOD AND DRINKS

PLANS FOR TODAY

1. ....
2. ....
3. ....

MY BEST EXPERIENCE TODAY

EVENING EVENTS

NEW FRIENDS

NOTES

Day # .... Place ....

DATE

TEMPERATURE

☐ **PORT**   ☐ **AT SEA**

SHIPBOARD ACTIVITIES LIST

FOOD AND DRINKS

PLANS FOR TODAY

1. ....
2. ....
3. ....

MY BEST EXPERIENCE TODAY

EVENING EVENTS

NEW FRIENDS

NOTES

Day # .... Place ....

DATE

TEMPERATURE

☐ PORT   ☐ AT SEA

SHIPBOARD ACTIVITIES LIST

FOOD AND DRINKS

PLANS FOR TODAY

1. ....
2. ....
3. ....

MY BEST EXPERIENCE TODAY

EVENING EVENTS

NEW FRIENDS

NOTES

Day # .... Place ....

DATE

TEMPERATURE

☐ PORT   ☐ AT SEA

SHIPBOARD ACTIVITIES LIST

FOOD AND DRINKS

PLANS FOR TODAY

1. ....
2. ....
3. ....

MY BEST EXPERIENCE TODAY

EVENING EVENTS

NEW FRIENDS

NOTES

Day # .... Place ....

DATE

TEMPERATURE

☐ **PORT**   ☐ **AT SEA**

SHIPBOARD ACTIVITIES LIST

....
....
....

FOOD AND DRINKS

PLANS FOR TODAY

1. ....
2. ....
3. ....

MY BEST EXPERIENCE TODAY

....
....
....
....

EVENING EVENTS

....
....
....

NEW FRIENDS

NOTES

....
....
....

Day # .... Place ....

DATE

TEMPERATURE

☐ PORT　　☐ AT SEA

SHIPBOARD ACTIVITIES LIST

FOOD AND DRINKS

PLANS FOR TODAY

1. ....
2. ....
3. ....

MY BEST EXPERIENCE TODAY

EVENING EVENTS

NEW FRIENDS

NOTES

Day # .... Place ....

DATE	
TEMPERATURE	

☐ PORT ☐ AT SEA

SHIPBOARD ACTIVITIES LIST

FOOD AND DRINKS

PLANS FOR TODAY

1. ....
2. ....
3. ....

MY BEST EXPERIENCE TODAY

EVENING EVENTS

NEW FRIENDS

NOTES

Day # .... Place ....

DATE

TEMPERATURE

☐ PORT ☐ AT SEA

SHIPBOARD ACTIVITIES LIST

FOOD AND DRINKS

PLANS FOR TODAY

1. ....
2. ....
3. ....

MY BEST EXPERIENCE TODAY

EVENING EVENTS

NEW FRIENDS

NOTES

Day # .... Place ....

DATE

TEMPERATURE

☐ PORT   ☐ AT SEA

SHIPBOARD ACTIVITIES LIST

FOOD AND DRINKS

PLANS FOR TODAY

1. ....
2. ....
3. ....

MY BEST EXPERIENCE TODAY

EVENING EVENTS

NEW FRIENDS

NOTES

Day # .... Place ....

DATE

TEMPERATURE

☐ PORT ☐ AT SEA

SHIPBOARD ACTIVITIES LIST

FOOD AND DRINKS

PLANS FOR TODAY

1. ....
2. ....
3. ....

MY BEST EXPERIENCE TODAY

EVENING EVENTS

NEW FRIENDS

NOTES

Day # .... Place ....

DATE

TEMPERATURE

☐ PORT   ☐ AT SEA

SHIPBOARD ACTIVITIES LIST

FOOD AND DRINKS

PLANS FOR TODAY

1. ....
2. ....
3. ....

MY BEST EXPERIENCE TODAY

EVENING EVENTS

NEW FRIENDS

NOTES

Day # .... Place ....

DATE

TEMPERATURE

☐ PORT   ☐ AT SEA

SHIPBOARD ACTIVITIES LIST

FOOD AND DRINKS

PLANS FOR TODAY

1. ....
2. ....
3. ....

MY BEST EXPERIENCE TODAY

EVENING EVENTS

NEW FRIENDS

NOTES

Day # .... Place ....

SHIPBOARD ACTIVITIES LIST

FOOD AND DRINKS

PLANS FOR TODAY

1. ....
2. ....
3. ....

MY BEST EXPERIENCE TODAY

EVENING EVENTS

NEW FRIENDS

NOTES

Day # .... Place ....

DATE

TEMPERATURE

☐ **PORT** ☐ **AT SEA**

SHIPBOARD ACTIVITIES LIST

FOOD AND DRINKS

PLANS FOR TODAY

1. ....
2. ....
3. ....

MY BEST EXPERIENCE TODAY

EVENING EVENTS

NEW FRIENDS

NOTES

Day # .... Place ....

DATE

TEMPERATURE

☐ PORT ☐ AT SEA

SHIPBOARD ACTIVITIES LIST

FOOD AND DRINKS

PLANS FOR TODAY

1. ....
2. ....
3. ....

MY BEST EXPERIENCE TODAY

EVENING EVENTS

NEW FRIENDS

NOTES

Day # .... Place ....

DATE

TEMPERATURE

☐ PORT ☐ AT SEA

SHIPBOARD ACTIVITIES LIST

FOOD AND DRINKS

PLANS FOR TODAY

1. ....
2. ....
3. ....

MY BEST EXPERIENCE TODAY

EVENING EVENTS

NEW FRIENDS

NOTES

Day # .... Place ....

DATE

TEMPERATURE

☐ PORT ☐ AT SEA

SHIPBOARD ACTIVITIES LIST

FOOD AND DRINKS

PLANS FOR TODAY

1. ....
2. ....
3. ....

MY BEST EXPERIENCE TODAY

EVENING EVENTS

NEW FRIENDS

NOTES

Day # .... Place ....

DATE

TEMPERATURE

☐ **PORT**   ☐ **AT SEA**

SHIPBOARD ACTIVITIES LIST

FOOD AND DRINKS

PLANS FOR TODAY

1. ....
2. ....
3. ....

MY BEST EXPERIENCE TODAY

EVENING EVENTS

NEW FRIENDS

NOTES

Day # .... Place ....

DATE	
TEMPERATURE	

☐ PORT   ☐ AT SEA

SHIPBOARD ACTIVITIES LIST

....
....
....

FOOD AND DRINKS

PLANS FOR TODAY

1. ....
2. ....
3. ....

MY BEST EXPERIENCE TODAY

....
....
....
....

EVENING EVENTS

....
....
....

NEW FRIENDS

NOTES

....
....
....

Day # .... Place ....

DATE

TEMPERATURE

☐ PORT   ☐ AT SEA

SHIPBOARD ACTIVITIES LIST

FOOD AND DRINKS

PLANS FOR TODAY

1. ....
2. ....
3. ....

MY BEST EXPERIENCE TODAY

EVENING EVENTS

NEW FRIENDS

NOTES

Day # .... Place ....

DATE

TEMPERATURE

☐ PORT ☐ AT SEA

SHIPBOARD ACTIVITIES LIST

FOOD AND DRINKS

PLANS FOR TODAY

1. ....
2. ....
3. ....

MY BEST EXPERIENCE TODAY

EVENING EVENTS

NEW FRIENDS

NOTES

Day # .... Place ....

DATE

TEMPERATURE

☐ **PORT** ☐ **AT SEA**

SHIPBOARD ACTIVITIES LIST

FOOD AND DRINKS

PLANS FOR TODAY

1. ....
2. ....
3. ....

MY BEST EXPERIENCE TODAY

EVENING EVENTS

NEW FRIENDS

NOTES

Day # .... Place ....

DATE

TEMPERATURE

☐ PORT   ☐ AT SEA

SHIPBOARD ACTIVITIES LIST

FOOD AND DRINKS

PLANS FOR TODAY

1. ....
2. ....
3. ....

MY BEST EXPERIENCE TODAY

EVENING EVENTS

NEW FRIENDS

NOTES

Day # .... Place ....

DATE

TEMPERATURE

☐ PORT   ☐ AT SEA

SHIPBOARD ACTIVITIES LIST

FOOD AND DRINKS

PLANS FOR TODAY

1. ....
2. ....
3. ....

MY BEST EXPERIENCE TODAY

EVENING EVENTS

NEW FRIENDS

NOTES

Day # .... Place ....

DATE

TEMPERATURE

☐ PORT ☐ AT SEA

SHIPBOARD ACTIVITIES LIST

FOOD AND DRINKS

PLANS FOR TODAY

1. ....
2. ....
3. ....

MY BEST EXPERIENCE TODAY

EVENING EVENTS

NEW FRIENDS

NOTES

Day # .... Place ....

DATE

TEMPERATURE

☐ PORT   ☐ AT SEA

SHIPBOARD ACTIVITIES LIST

FOOD AND DRINKS

PLANS FOR TODAY

1. ....
2. ....
3. ....

MY BEST EXPERIENCE TODAY

EVENING EVENTS

NEW FRIENDS

NOTES

Day # .... Place ....

DATE

TEMPERATURE

☐ PORT ☐ AT SEA

SHIPBOARD ACTIVITIES LIST

FOOD AND DRINKS

PLANS FOR TODAY

1. ....
2. ....
3. ....

MY BEST EXPERIENCE TODAY

EVENING EVENTS

NEW FRIENDS

NOTES

Day # .... Place ....

DATE

TEMPERATURE

☐ PORT ☐ AT SEA

SHIPBOARD ACTIVITIES LIST

....
....
....

FOOD AND DRINKS

PLANS FOR TODAY

1. ....
2. ....
3. ....

MY BEST EXPERIENCE TODAY

....
....
....
....

EVENING EVENTS

....
....
....

NEW FRIENDS

NOTES

....
....
....

Day # .... Place ....

DATE

TEMPERATURE

☐ **PORT**   ☐ **AT SEA**

SHIPBOARD ACTIVITIES LIST

....
....
....

FOOD AND DRINKS

PLANS FOR TODAY

1. ....
2. ....
3. ....

MY BEST EXPERIENCE TODAY

....
....
....
....

EVENING EVENTS

....
....
....

NEW FRIENDS

NOTES

....
....
....

Day # .... Place ....

DATE

TEMPERATURE

☐ **PORT**   ☐ **AT SEA**

SHIPBOARD ACTIVITIES LIST

FOOD AND DRINKS

PLANS FOR TODAY

1. ....
2. ....
3. ....

MY BEST EXPERIENCE TODAY

EVENING EVENTS

NEW FRIENDS

NOTES

Day # .... Place ....

DATE

TEMPERATURE

☐ PORT   ☐ AT SEA

SHIPBOARD ACTIVITIES LIST

FOOD AND DRINKS

PLANS FOR TODAY

1. ....
2. ....
3. ....

MY BEST EXPERIENCE TODAY

EVENING EVENTS

NEW FRIENDS

NOTES

Day # .... Place ....

DATE

TEMPERATURE

☐ PORT ☐ AT SEA

SHIPBOARD ACTIVITIES LIST

FOOD AND DRINKS

PLANS FOR TODAY

1. ....
2. ....
3. ....

MY BEST EXPERIENCE TODAY

EVENING EVENTS

NEW FRIENDS

NOTES

Day # .... Place ....

<table>
<tr><td>

DATE

TEMPERATURE

☐ **PORT** ☐ **AT SEA**

</td><td>

SHIPBOARD ACTIVITIES LIST

</td></tr>
</table>

FOOD AND DRINKS

PLANS FOR TODAY

1. ....
2. ....
3. ....

MY BEST EXPERIENCE TODAY

EVENING EVENTS

NEW FRIENDS

NOTES

Day # .... Place ....

DATE	
TEMPERATURE	

☐ **PORT**   ☐ **AT SEA**

SHIPBOARD ACTIVITIES LIST

....
....
....

FOOD AND DRINKS

PLANS FOR TODAY

1. ....
2. ....
3. ....

MY BEST EXPERIENCE TODAY

....
....
....
....

EVENING EVENTS

....
....
....

NEW FRIENDS

NOTES

....
....
....

Day # .... Place ....

DATE

TEMPERATURE

☐ PORT   ☐ AT SEA

SHIPBOARD ACTIVITIES LIST

FOOD AND DRINKS

PLANS FOR TODAY

1. ....
2. ....
3. ....

MY BEST EXPERIENCE TODAY

EVENING EVENTS

NEW FRIENDS

NOTES

Day # .... Place ....

DATE

TEMPERATURE

☐ PORT ☐ AT SEA

SHIPBOARD ACTIVITIES LIST

FOOD AND DRINKS

PLANS FOR TODAY

1. ....
2. ....
3. ....

MY BEST EXPERIENCE TODAY

EVENING EVENTS

NEW FRIENDS

NOTES

Day # .... Place ....

DATE

TEMPERATURE

☐ **PORT** ☐ **AT SEA**

SHIPBOARD ACTIVITIES LIST

FOOD AND DRINKS

PLANS FOR TODAY

1. ....
2. ....
3. ....

MY BEST EXPERIENCE TODAY

EVENING EVENTS

NEW FRIENDS

NOTES

Day # .... Place ....

DATE

TEMPERATURE

☐ PORT   ☐ AT SEA

SHIPBOARD ACTIVITIES LIST

FOOD AND DRINKS

PLANS FOR TODAY

1. ....
2. ....
3. ....

MY BEST EXPERIENCE TODAY

EVENING EVENTS

NEW FRIENDS

NOTES

Day # .... Place ....

DATE

TEMPERATURE

☐ PORT   ☐ AT SEA

SHIPBOARD ACTIVITIES LIST

FOOD AND DRINKS

PLANS FOR TODAY

1. ....
2. ....
3. ....

MY BEST EXPERIENCE TODAY

EVENING EVENTS

NEW FRIENDS

NOTES

Day # .... Place ....

DATE

TEMPERATURE

☐ PORT   ☐ AT SEA

SHIPBOARD ACTIVITIES LIST

FOOD AND DRINKS

PLANS FOR TODAY

1. ....
2. ....
3. ....

MY BEST EXPERIENCE TODAY

EVENING EVENTS

NEW FRIENDS

NOTES

Day # .... Place ....

DATE

TEMPERATURE

☐ **PORT** ☐ **AT SEA**

SHIPBOARD ACTIVITIES LIST

FOOD AND DRINKS

PLANS FOR TODAY

1. ....
2. ....
3. ....

MY BEST EXPERIENCE TODAY

EVENING EVENTS

NEW FRIENDS

NOTES

Day # .... Place ....

DATE

TEMPERATURE

☐ PORT   ☐ AT SEA

SHIPBOARD ACTIVITIES LIST

FOOD AND DRINKS

PLANS FOR TODAY

1. ....
2. ....
3. ....

MY BEST EXPERIENCE TODAY

EVENING EVENTS

NEW FRIENDS

NOTES

Day # .... Place ....

DATE

TEMPERATURE

☐ PORT   ☐ AT SEA

SHIPBOARD ACTIVITIES LIST

FOOD AND DRINKS

PLANS FOR TODAY

1. ....
2. ....
3. ....

MY BEST EXPERIENCE TODAY

EVENING EVENTS

NEW FRIENDS

NOTES

Day # .... Place ....

DATE

TEMPERATURE

☐ PORT   ☐ AT SEA

SHIPBOARD ACTIVITIES LIST

....
....
....

FOOD AND DRINKS

PLANS FOR TODAY

1. ....
2. ....
3. ....

MY BEST EXPERIENCE TODAY

....
....
....
....

EVENING EVENTS

....
....
....

NEW FRIENDS

NOTES

....
....
....

Day # .... Place ....

DATE

TEMPERATURE

☐ **PORT**   ☐ **AT SEA**

SHIPBOARD ACTIVITIES LIST

....
....
....

FOOD AND DRINKS

PLANS FOR TODAY

1. ....
2. ....
3. ....

MY BEST EXPERIENCE TODAY

....
....
....
....

EVENING EVENTS

....
....
....

NEW FRIENDS

NOTES

....
....
....

Day # .... Place ....

DATE

TEMPERATURE

☐ PORT   ☐ AT SEA

SHIPBOARD ACTIVITIES LIST

....
....
....

FOOD AND DRINKS

PLANS FOR TODAY

1. ....
2. ....
3. ....

MY BEST EXPERIENCE TODAY

....
....
....
....

EVENING EVENTS

....
....
....

NEW FRIENDS

NOTES

....
....
....

Day # .... Place ....

DATE	
TEMPERATURE	

☐ PORT   ☐ AT SEA

SHIPBOARD ACTIVITIES LIST

....

....

....

FOOD AND DRINKS

PLANS FOR TODAY

1. ....
2. ....
3. ....

MY BEST EXPERIENCE TODAY

....

....

....

....

EVENING EVENTS

....

....

....

NEW FRIENDS

NOTES

....

....

....

Day # .... Place ....

DATE

TEMPERATURE

☐ PORT ☐ AT SEA

SHIPBOARD ACTIVITIES LIST

FOOD AND DRINKS

PLANS FOR TODAY

1. ....
2. ....
3. ....

MY BEST EXPERIENCE TODAY

EVENING EVENTS

NEW FRIENDS

NOTES

Day # .... Place ....

DATE

TEMPERATURE

☐ PORT   ☐ AT SEA

SHIPBOARD ACTIVITIES LIST

FOOD AND DRINKS

PLANS FOR TODAY

1. ....
2. ....
3. ....

MY BEST EXPERIENCE TODAY

EVENING EVENTS

NEW FRIENDS

NOTES

Day # .... Place ....

DATE

TEMPERATURE

☐ PORT   ☐ AT SEA

SHIPBOARD ACTIVITIES LIST

FOOD AND DRINKS

PLANS FOR TODAY

1. ....
2. ....
3. ....

MY BEST EXPERIENCE TODAY

EVENING EVENTS

NEW FRIENDS

NOTES

Day # .... Place ....

DATE

TEMPERATURE

☐ **PORT**   ☐ **AT SEA**

SHIPBOARD ACTIVITIES LIST

FOOD AND DRINKS

PLANS FOR TODAY

1. ....
2. ....
3. ....

MY BEST EXPERIENCE TODAY

EVENING EVENTS

NEW FRIENDS

NOTES

Day # .... Place ....

DATE

TEMPERATURE

☐ PORT ☐ AT SEA

SHIPBOARD ACTIVITIES LIST

FOOD AND DRINKS

PLANS FOR TODAY

1. ....
2. ....
3. ....

MY BEST EXPERIENCE TODAY

EVENING EVENTS

NEW FRIENDS

NOTES

Day # .... Place ....

DATE

TEMPERATURE

☐ **PORT**   ☐ **AT SEA**

SHIPBOARD ACTIVITIES LIST

FOOD AND DRINKS

PLANS FOR TODAY

1. ....
2. ....
3. ....

MY BEST EXPERIENCE TODAY

EVENING EVENTS

NEW FRIENDS

NOTES

Day # .... Place ....

DATE

TEMPERATURE

☐ PORT ☐ AT SEA

SHIPBOARD ACTIVITIES LIST

FOOD AND DRINKS

PLANS FOR TODAY

1. ....
2. ....
3. ....

MY BEST EXPERIENCE TODAY

EVENING EVENTS

NEW FRIENDS

NOTES

Day # .... Place ....

DATE

TEMPERATURE

☐ PORT ☐ AT SEA

SHIPBOARD ACTIVITIES LIST

FOOD AND DRINKS

PLANS FOR TODAY

1. ....
2. ....
3. ....

MY BEST EXPERIENCE TODAY

EVENING EVENTS

NEW FRIENDS

NOTES

Day # .... Place ....

DATE

TEMPERATURE

☐ PORT   ☐ AT SEA

SHIPBOARD ACTIVITIES LIST

FOOD AND DRINKS

PLANS FOR TODAY

1. ....
2. ....
3. ....

MY BEST EXPERIENCE TODAY

EVENING EVENTS

NEW FRIENDS

NOTES

Day # .... Place ....

DATE

TEMPERATURE

☐ PORT   ☐ AT SEA

SHIPBOARD ACTIVITIES LIST

FOOD AND DRINKS

PLANS FOR TODAY

1. ....
2. ....
3. ....

MY BEST EXPERIENCE TODAY

EVENING EVENTS

NEW FRIENDS

NOTES

Day # .... Place ....

DATE

TEMPERATURE

☐ **PORT**   ☐ **AT SEA**

SHIPBOARD ACTIVITIES LIST

FOOD AND DRINKS

PLANS FOR TODAY

1. ....
2. ....
3. ....

MY BEST EXPERIENCE TODAY

EVENING EVENTS

NEW FRIENDS

NOTES

Day # .... Place ....

DATE

TEMPERATURE

☐ PORT ☐ AT SEA

SHIPBOARD ACTIVITIES LIST

FOOD AND DRINKS

PLANS FOR TODAY

1. ....
2. ....
3. ....

MY BEST EXPERIENCE TODAY

EVENING EVENTS

NEW FRIENDS

NOTES

Day # .... Place ....

DATE

TEMPERATURE

☐ PORT   ☐ AT SEA

SHIPBOARD ACTIVITIES LIST

FOOD AND DRINKS

PLANS FOR TODAY

1. ....
2. ....
3. ....

MY BEST EXPERIENCE TODAY

EVENING EVENTS

NEW FRIENDS

NOTES

Day # .... Place ....

DATE

TEMPERATURE

☐ **PORT**   ☐ **AT SEA**

SHIPBOARD ACTIVITIES LIST

FOOD AND DRINKS

PLANS FOR TODAY

1. ....
2. ....
3. ....

MY BEST EXPERIENCE TODAY

EVENING EVENTS

NEW FRIENDS

NOTES

Day # .... Place ....

DATE

TEMPERATURE

☐ PORT   ☐ AT SEA

SHIPBOARD ACTIVITIES LIST

FOOD AND DRINKS

PLANS FOR TODAY

1. ....
2. ....
3. ....

MY BEST EXPERIENCE TODAY

EVENING EVENTS

NEW FRIENDS

NOTES

Day # .... Place ....

DATE

TEMPERATURE

☐ PORT   ☐ AT SEA

SHIPBOARD ACTIVITIES LIST

FOOD AND DRINKS

PLANS FOR TODAY

1. ....
2. ....
3. ....

MY BEST EXPERIENCE TODAY

EVENING EVENTS

NEW FRIENDS

NOTES

Day # .... Place ....

DATE

TEMPERATURE

☐ PORT   ☐ AT SEA

SHIPBOARD ACTIVITIES LIST

FOOD AND DRINKS

PLANS FOR TODAY

1. ....
2. ....
3. ....

MY BEST EXPERIENCE TODAY

EVENING EVENTS

NEW FRIENDS

NOTES

Day # .... Place ....

DATE

TEMPERATURE

☐ **PORT**   ☐ **AT SEA**

SHIPBOARD ACTIVITIES LIST

FOOD AND DRINKS

PLANS FOR TODAY

1. ....
2. ....
3. ....

MY BEST EXPERIENCE TODAY

EVENING EVENTS

NEW FRIENDS

NOTES

Day # .... Place ....

DATE

TEMPERATURE

☐ **PORT** ☐ **AT SEA**

SHIPBOARD ACTIVITIES LIST

FOOD AND DRINKS

PLANS FOR TODAY

1. ....
2. ....
3. ....

MY BEST EXPERIENCE TODAY

EVENING EVENTS

NEW FRIENDS

NOTES

Day # .... Place ....

DATE

TEMPERATURE

☐ PORT   ☐ AT SEA

SHIPBOARD ACTIVITIES LIST

FOOD AND DRINKS

PLANS FOR TODAY

1. ....
2. ....
3. ....

MY BEST EXPERIENCE TODAY

EVENING EVENTS

NEW FRIENDS

NOTES

Day # .... Place ....

DATE

TEMPERATURE

☐ PORT ☐ AT SEA

SHIPBOARD ACTIVITIES LIST

FOOD AND DRINKS

PLANS FOR TODAY

1. ....
2. ....
3. ....

MY BEST EXPERIENCE TODAY

EVENING EVENTS

NEW FRIENDS

NOTES

Day #   Place

DATE

TEMPERATURE

☐ PORT   ☐ AT SEA

SHIPBOARD ACTIVITIES LIST

FOOD AND DRINKS

PLANS FOR TODAY

1.
2.
3.

MY BEST EXPERIENCE TODAY

EVENING EVENTS

NEW FRIENDS

NOTES

Day # .... Place ....

DATE

TEMPERATURE

☐ PORT ☐ AT SEA

SHIPBOARD ACTIVITIES LIST

FOOD AND DRINKS

PLANS FOR TODAY

1. ....
2. ....
3. ....

MY BEST EXPERIENCE TODAY

EVENING EVENTS

NEW FRIENDS

NOTES

Day # .... Place ....

DATE

TEMPERATURE

☐ PORT ☐ AT SEA

SHIPBOARD ACTIVITIES LIST

FOOD AND DRINKS

PLANS FOR TODAY

1. ....
2. ....
3. ....

MY BEST EXPERIENCE TODAY

EVENING EVENTS

NEW FRIENDS

NOTES

Day # .... Place ....

SHIPBOARD ACTIVITIES LIST

FOOD AND DRINKS

PLANS FOR TODAY

1. ....
2. ....
3. ....

MY BEST EXPERIENCE TODAY

EVENING EVENTS

NEW FRIENDS

NOTES

Day # .... Place ....

DATE

TEMPERATURE

☐ PORT   ☐ AT SEA

SHIPBOARD ACTIVITIES LIST

FOOD AND DRINKS

PLANS FOR TODAY

1. ....
2. ....
3. ....

MY BEST EXPERIENCE TODAY

EVENING EVENTS

NEW FRIENDS

NOTES

Day # .... Place ....

DATE

TEMPERATURE

☐ PORT ☐ AT SEA

SHIPBOARD ACTIVITIES LIST

FOOD AND DRINKS

PLANS FOR TODAY

1. ....
2. ....
3. ....

MY BEST EXPERIENCE TODAY

EVENING EVENTS

NEW FRIENDS

NOTES

Day # .... Place ....

DATE

TEMPERATURE

☐ PORT   ☐ AT SEA

SHIPBOARD ACTIVITIES LIST

....

....

....

FOOD AND DRINKS

PLANS FOR TODAY

1. ....
2. ....
3. ....

MY BEST EXPERIENCE TODAY

....

....

....

....

EVENING EVENTS

....

....

....

NEW FRIENDS

NOTES

....

....

....

Day # .... Place ....

DATE

TEMPERATURE

☐ PORT ☐ AT SEA

SHIPBOARD ACTIVITIES LIST

FOOD AND DRINKS

PLANS FOR TODAY

1. ....
2. ....
3. ....

MY BEST EXPERIENCE TODAY

EVENING EVENTS

NEW FRIENDS

NOTES

Day # .... Place ....

DATE

TEMPERATURE

☐ **PORT**　　☐ **AT SEA**

SHIPBOARD ACTIVITIES LIST

FOOD AND DRINKS

PLANS FOR TODAY

1. ....
2. ....
3. ....

MY BEST EXPERIENCE TODAY

EVENING EVENTS

NEW FRIENDS

NOTES

Day # .... Place ....

DATE

TEMPERATURE

☐ PORT ☐ AT SEA

SHIPBOARD ACTIVITIES LIST

FOOD AND DRINKS

PLANS FOR TODAY

1. ....
2. ....
3. ....

MY BEST EXPERIENCE TODAY

EVENING EVENTS

NEW FRIENDS

NOTES

Day # .... Place ....

DATE

TEMPERATURE

☐ PORT   ☐ AT SEA

SHIPBOARD ACTIVITIES LIST

FOOD AND DRINKS

PLANS FOR TODAY

1. ....
2. ....
3. ....

MY BEST EXPERIENCE TODAY

EVENING EVENTS

NEW FRIENDS

NOTES

Day # .... Place ....

SHIPBOARD ACTIVITIES LIST

....
....
....

FOOD AND DRINKS

PLANS FOR TODAY

1. ....
2. ....
3. ....

MY BEST EXPERIENCE TODAY

....
....
....
....

EVENING EVENTS

....
....
....

NEW FRIENDS

NOTES

....
....
....

Day # .... Place ....

DATE

TEMPERATURE

☐ **PORT**   ☐ **AT SEA**

SHIPBOARD ACTIVITIES LIST

FOOD AND DRINKS

PLANS FOR TODAY

1. ....
2. ....
3. ....

MY BEST EXPERIENCE TODAY

EVENING EVENTS

NEW FRIENDS

NOTES

Day # .... Place ....

DATE

TEMPERATURE

☐ PORT   ☐ AT SEA

SHIPBOARD ACTIVITIES LIST

FOOD AND DRINKS

PLANS FOR TODAY

1. ....
2. ....
3. ....

MY BEST EXPERIENCE TODAY

EVENING EVENTS

NEW FRIENDS

NOTES

Day # .... Place ....

SHIPBOARD ACTIVITIES LIST

FOOD AND DRINKS

PLANS FOR TODAY

1. ....
2. ....
3. ....

MY BEST EXPERIENCE TODAY

EVENING EVENTS

NEW FRIENDS

NOTES

Day # .... Place ....

DATE

TEMPERATURE

☐ PORT   ☐ AT SEA

SHIPBOARD ACTIVITIES LIST

FOOD AND DRINKS

PLANS FOR TODAY

1. ....
2. ....
3. ....

MY BEST EXPERIENCE TODAY

EVENING EVENTS

NEW FRIENDS

NOTES

Day #   Place

DATE

TEMPERATURE

☐ **PORT**   ☐ **AT SEA**

SHIPBOARD ACTIVITIES LIST

FOOD AND DRINKS

PLANS FOR TODAY

1.
2.
3.

MY BEST EXPERIENCE TODAY

EVENING EVENTS

NEW FRIENDS

NOTES

Day # .... Place ....

DATE

TEMPERATURE

☐ PORT   ☐ AT SEA

SHIPBOARD ACTIVITIES LIST

....
....
....

FOOD AND DRINKS

PLANS FOR TODAY

1. ....
2. ....
3. ....

MY BEST EXPERIENCE TODAY

....
....
....
....

EVENING EVENTS

....
....
....

NEW FRIENDS

NOTES

....
....
....

Day # .... Place ....

DATE

TEMPERATURE

☐ PORT ☐ AT SEA

SHIPBOARD ACTIVITIES LIST

FOOD AND DRINKS

PLANS FOR TODAY

1. ....
2. ....
3. ....

MY BEST EXPERIENCE TODAY

EVENING EVENTS

NEW FRIENDS

NOTES

Day # .... Place ....

DATE

TEMPERATURE

☐ PORT ☐ AT SEA

SHIPBOARD ACTIVITIES LIST

FOOD AND DRINKS

PLANS FOR TODAY

1. ....
2. ....
3. ....

MY BEST EXPERIENCE TODAY

EVENING EVENTS

NEW FRIENDS

NOTES

Day # .... Place ....

DATE

TEMPERATURE

☐ **PORT**   ☐ **AT SEA**

SHIPBOARD ACTIVITIES LIST

FOOD AND DRINKS

PLANS FOR TODAY

1. ....
2. ....
3. ....

MY BEST EXPERIENCE TODAY

EVENING EVENTS

NEW FRIENDS

NOTES

Day # .... Place ....

DATE

TEMPERATURE

☐ PORT   ☐ AT SEA

SHIPBOARD ACTIVITIES LIST

....
....
....

FOOD AND DRINKS

PLANS FOR TODAY

1. ....
2. ....
3. ....

MY BEST EXPERIENCE TODAY

....
....
....
....

EVENING EVENTS

....
....
....

NEW FRIENDS

NOTES

....
....
....

Day # .... Place ....

DATE

TEMPERATURE

☐ PORT   ☐ AT SEA

SHIPBOARD ACTIVITIES LIST

FOOD AND DRINKS

PLANS FOR TODAY

1. ....
2. ....
3. ....

MY BEST EXPERIENCE TODAY

EVENING EVENTS

NEW FRIENDS

NOTES

Day # .... Place ....

SHIPBOARD ACTIVITIES LIST

....
....
....

FOOD AND DRINKS

PLANS FOR TODAY

1. ....
2. ....
3. ....

MY BEST EXPERIENCE TODAY

....
....
....
....

EVENING EVENTS

....
....
....

NEW FRIENDS

NOTES

....
....
....

Day # .... Place ....

DATE

TEMPERATURE

☐ PORT   ☐ AT SEA

SHIPBOARD ACTIVITIES LIST

FOOD AND DRINKS

PLANS FOR TODAY

1. ....
2. ....
3. ....

MY BEST EXPERIENCE TODAY

EVENING EVENTS

NEW FRIENDS

NOTES

Day # .... Place ....

DATE

TEMPERATURE

☐ PORT   ☐ AT SEA

SHIPBOARD ACTIVITIES LIST

FOOD AND DRINKS

PLANS FOR TODAY

1. ....
2. ....
3. ....

MY BEST EXPERIENCE TODAY

EVENING EVENTS

NEW FRIENDS

NOTES

Day #　　　　Place

DATE

TEMPERATURE

☐ PORT　　☐ AT SEA

SHIPBOARD ACTIVITIES LIST

FOOD AND DRINKS

PLANS FOR TODAY

1.
2.
3.

MY BEST EXPERIENCE TODAY

EVENING EVENTS

NEW FRIENDS

NOTES

Day # .... Place ....

DATE

TEMPERATURE

☐ PORT ☐ AT SEA

SHIPBOARD ACTIVITIES LIST

....
....
....

FOOD AND DRINKS

PLANS FOR TODAY

1. ....
2. ....
3. ....

MY BEST EXPERIENCE TODAY

....
....
....
....

EVENING EVENTS

....
....
....

NEW FRIENDS

NOTES

....
....
....

Day # .... Place ....

DATE

TEMPERATURE

☐ PORT   ☐ AT SEA

SHIPBOARD ACTIVITIES LIST

....
....
....

FOOD AND DRINKS

PLANS FOR TODAY

1. ....
2. ....
3. ....

MY BEST EXPERIENCE TODAY

....
....
....
....

EVENING EVENTS

....
....
....

NEW FRIENDS

NOTES

....
....
....

Day # .... Place ....

DATE

TEMPERATURE

☐ PORT ☐ AT SEA

SHIPBOARD ACTIVITIES LIST

FOOD AND DRINKS

PLANS FOR TODAY

1. ....
2. ....
3. ....

MY BEST EXPERIENCE TODAY

EVENING EVENTS

NEW FRIENDS

NOTES

Day # .... Place ....

DATE

TEMPERATURE

☐ PORT   ☐ AT SEA

SHIPBOARD ACTIVITIES LIST

FOOD AND DRINKS

PLANS FOR TODAY

1. ....
2. ....
3. ....

MY BEST EXPERIENCE TODAY

EVENING EVENTS

NEW FRIENDS

NOTES

Day # .... Place ....

DATE

TEMPERATURE

☐ PORT   ☐ AT SEA

SHIPBOARD ACTIVITIES LIST

....
....
....

FOOD AND DRINKS

PLANS FOR TODAY

1. ....
2. ....
3. ....

MY BEST EXPERIENCE TODAY

....
....
....
....

EVENING EVENTS

....
....
....

NEW FRIENDS

NOTES

....
....
....

Day # .... Place ....

DATE

TEMPERATURE

☐ PORT ☐ AT SEA

SHIPBOARD ACTIVITIES LIST

FOOD AND DRINKS

PLANS FOR TODAY

1. ....
2. ....
3. ....

MY BEST EXPERIENCE TODAY

EVENING EVENTS

NEW FRIENDS

NOTES

Day # .... Place ....

DATE

TEMPERATURE

☐ PORT ☐ AT SEA

SHIPBOARD ACTIVITIES LIST

FOOD AND DRINKS

PLANS FOR TODAY

1. ....
2. ....
3. ....

MY BEST EXPERIENCE TODAY

EVENING EVENTS

NEW FRIENDS

NOTES

Day # .... Place ....

DATE

TEMPERATURE

☐ PORT   ☐ AT SEA

SHIPBOARD ACTIVITIES LIST

FOOD AND DRINKS

PLANS FOR TODAY

1. ....
2. ....
3. ....

MY BEST EXPERIENCE TODAY

EVENING EVENTS

NEW FRIENDS

NOTES

Day # .... Place ....

☐ PORT ☐ AT SEA

SHIPBOARD ACTIVITIES LIST

FOOD AND DRINKS

PLANS FOR TODAY

1. ....
2. ....
3. ....

MY BEST EXPERIENCE TODAY

EVENING EVENTS

NEW FRIENDS

NOTES

www.ingramcontent.com/pod-product-compliance
Lightning Source LLC
LaVergne TN
LVHW060354200726
843506LV00003B/212